CELTIC ALPHABETS

Aidan Meehan was born in 1951 in Northern Ireland, and educated in Newry and at Queen's University, Belfast. After leaving Ireland in 1973, he discovered a deep interest in Celtic design, which led to his eight-volume *Celtic Design Series* and

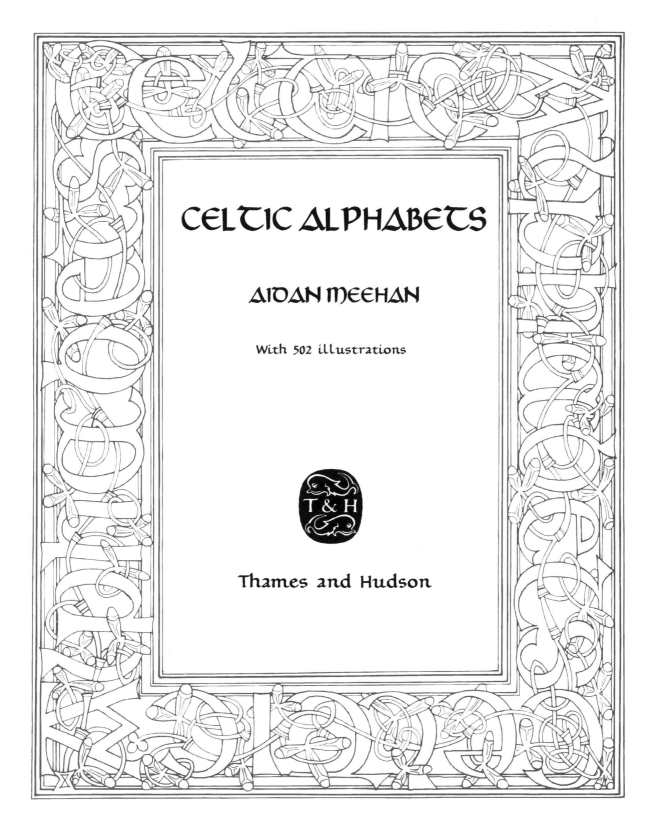

CELTIC ALPHABETS

AIDAN MEEHAN

With 502 illustrations

Thames and Hudson

For Finola

British Library Cataloguing-in-Publication Data

A catalogue record for this book is available from the
British Library

ISBN 0-500-27980-2

Printed and bound in Spain

Contents

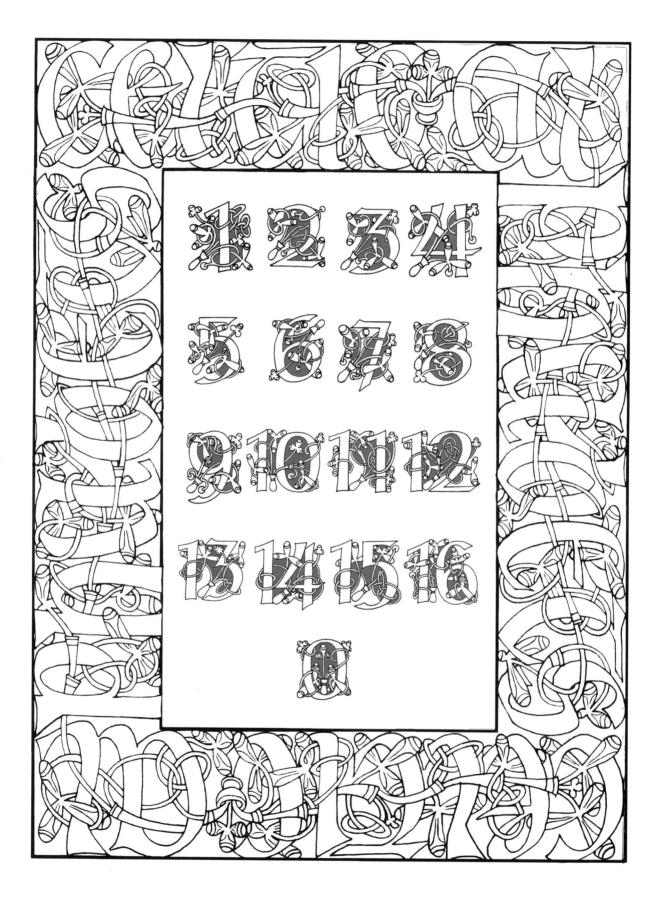

THIS BOOK is one I had in mind for over a decade, developing the idea throughout the *Celtic Design* series. The decorated letter is the main application of Celtic art, and so it seemed natural to explore ornamental letters, not only in the book on *Illuminated Letters*, but in the decoration of all the other books in the series.

While searching The Book of Kells for examples of illuminated letters, I discovered an almost complete alphabet of lions. Almost complete, because some letters do not happen to occur in the text, and others such as J, K, L, W had not yet come into general use. There were more than enough there, though, to suggest that a complete alphabet had once existed, and that such an alphabet of animal letters could be usefully reinvented by a modern scribe.

Introduction

Again in *Illuminated Letters*, I collected ampersands, or "&s", of very varied design, some with lions and birds, but mostly serpentine fish forms. These last perhaps represented the germ of another new alphabet, never completed. From these examples, I imagined that a whole alphabet of interlaced eels could be re-created, given a knowledge of the letterforms of the time (see *Alphabet 8: Eels*).

These letterforms were easily found. Large black letters in Irish Majuscule were used extensively in manuscripts of the period, decorated with all kinds of Celtic designs. Sometimes two or three share the same motifs, so well-matched as to suggest other complete alphabets, such as might once have been collected in a Celtic ABC book copied from library to library. No example of such a book has survived, but collections of alphabets are likely to have existed as textbooks in a school of scribes. Celtic artists today would find such a manual extremely valuable, should one ever be discovered.

I felt in the meantime that I could assemble such a set of alphabets, adapted to the modern alphabet and complete. This would supply the modern designer with a reference for a particular letter in a particular Celtic style of ornament – knotwork, animal, spiral, maze or plant – where perhaps it might be missing from the surviving sources.

In making my own books, from the beginning I designed
decorated initials to lead into each chapter, starting with
individual letters, each different, and as the series
progressed the initials all took on a family resemblance, as
if they belonged to the same alphabet, although at the time I
was just designing each as required for the text. You can
see some examples of these early experiments on the
following pages, *figs* 1 and 2. They are taken from the first
six books of the *Celtic Design* series. In the seventh, I used
letters from the animal alphabet of *Illuminated Letters*, and
then felt a need for a complete alphabet. In *The Tree of Life*,
I designed an alphabet based on modern capitals, decorated
with eel knots – *Alphabet 1: Eel Caps* – the first alphabet in
this book. *Alphabet 2: Cathach* (pronounced "Ca-hak"),
which is called after the famous manuscript of that name,
returns to Celtic script, as do the remaining alphabets.
Alphabet 3: Spirals is modelled on the Book of Durrow;
Alphabet 4: Bird Head on the Book of Durham; and
Alphabet 5: Dog Head is modelled on the Book of Lindisfarne.
The rest are based on letters from The Book of Kells, except
for the last, which is based on the 12th-century Harley
manuscript. Since *The Dragon and the Griffin* is the only book
in the series without its own initials, I have called this
final alphabet *Draco*. Many of these alphabets have been
given a second colour, reminiscent of the red-painted letters
or "rubrication" of illuminated manuscripts.

Fig. 1: Decorative Initials from the Celtic Design Series

Four letters from "A Beginner's Manual"

Four letters from "Knotwork"

Four letters from "Animal Patterns"

Fig. 2: Decorative Initials from the Celtic Design Series

Four letters from "Illuminated Letters"

Four letters from "Spiral Patterns"

Four letters from "Maze Patterns"

Fig. 3: Decorative Initials from the Celtic Design Series

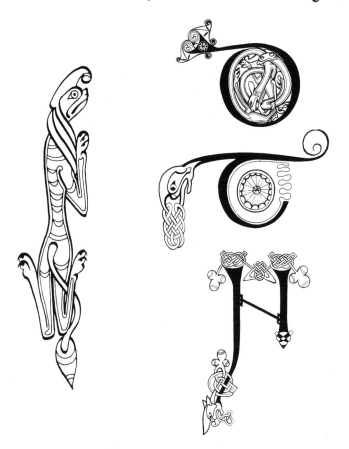

Four letters from "The Dragon and the Griffin"

Four letters from "The Tree of Life"

As I mentioned, the Book of Kells has a great number of
letters based on animal patterns, and the lion was clearly a
favourite choice. While I was collecting all the examples
of letters from the Book of Kells that I could find for
the animal alphabet chapter in *Illuminated Letters*, there
were so many more lions than birds or other creatures, I
began to think of it as a lion alphabet. Although it was in
fact missing quite a few letters, other letters that occurred
frequently were represented by half a dozen or so
examples. At one point, I suggested how some of the missing
letters could be made up to match any one of the existing
lion letters, although I left it to the reader to invent their
own letters G, W, X, Y, and Z. *Illuminated Letters* was
really a collection of studies from traditional sources,
but I also realized that the model I had suggested was
only one of many. Such a variety of alphabets could be
built on so many other examples from the animal alphabet
from this one manuscript, why single out just one?

Indeed, I was able to find all the initials I needed for
The Dragon and the Griffin from that animal alphabet alone.
It seemed to fit the subject of the book, in which the Viking
lion plays such a large role. However, as you can also see
on the previous page, the lions from the Book of Kells take
many forms. Some of them are whole animal figures
arranged to suggest letters, and others are black letters

with lions' heads attached to the ends of the pen strokes, as a decorative serif only. These two such different treatments work well in an illuminated manuscript filled with hundreds of different designs, but might not mix so well in the context of a single alphabet. Other letters are quite separate from their ornament, and just enclose a space with lions tied together inside, as pure decoration. It would be easy to imagine the centre part of the letter D, at the top of page 12, as having been taken from the design of a brooch or some other familiar object, adopted by the artist to fill the oval void of the letter.

This letter D in particular also has a fine spiral pattern decorating the serif. It inspired me to make *Alphabet 7 : Dogs*, in which I made the other letters of the alphabet to match it. Where some letters do not naturally enclose a space that could be filled with lions, I could use the spiral serifs to link the different kinds of letters together in the same alphabet. It seems a good idea to start off with two or three distinctive features that can be shared or alternated throughout a series in this way. I should mention in passing that although I was inspired by the lion, I also had in mind the dog which was used a lot in other manuscripts of the time, and the lion knot lent itself easily to the dog pattern I wanted to use.

In Celtic animal patterns, dogs and cats are interchangeable, being more or less the same shape, except that the dog has a longer nose and the lion has a tufted tail. While the lion seems to have been almost a trade mark of the Book of Kells, the dog was preferred in the Book of Lindisfarne. I like them both, so I have took the construction of the animals from the one book, and borrowed the style of drawing from the other.

While the lion letters from the Book of Kells easily suggest a whole alphabet on their own, it is quite a problem to try to complete such an alphabet. There are so many variations among the letters in the original, it seems that they were drawn from a number of alphabets, some with lions as secondary motifs, some with lion heads, and some all lions' bodies, so that several different alphabets suggest themselves. In fact, I found quite a few letters with a lion's head serif, and these together inspired *Alphabet 14: Lion Head*, so that I cannot say for certain that I had any particular letter in mind.

That is not to say the lion is the only animal head we can use to decorate a serif. In the Book of Kells, bird heads and human heads are used in the same way, even a rabbit head appears here and there, munching on a sprig. This appearance of the rabbit head was so startling to come across in the context that it always stuck in my mind as a most unusual treatment. It adds a touch of humour in otherwise serious surroundings. *Alphabet 13: Rabbit Head* may well serve the same purpose in this book.

The foliage which the Kells rabbit always seems to be nibbling suggested the Tree of Life to me, which is a motif I like to use a lot, and although there are very few examples of it used exclusively in a letter, I found one with a triangular knotwork serif with leaves sprouting from it that provided an excuse for *Alphabet 10: Trefoil*, and which I have used throughout this book for the chapter title pages, because it is such a pleasure to draw.

I liked another lion-head letter from the Book of Kells , also included in fig. 3, more for its abstract filler. This filler with a wavy line was also used without the animal head, with a simple, woven-line swash. This is the idea behind *Alphabet 9: Swash Knots.* I took this name from a kind of wavy line decoration used to embellish calligraphy since Renaissance times, and which I suppose had its origin in the Celtic manuscripts. Incidentally, similarly looping swash knots were still in widespread use until quite recently, as gold-braid trim on military uniforms, for example. In the eighteenth century such braid was nick-named "macaroni".

While lions were more often bent out of shape to make letters than any other animal form, they were not the only one, birds and human figures being the other main candidates in the Book of Kells, and dogs instead of human figures in the most other Celtic manuscripts. Towards the end of the making of the Book of Kells – the late eighth century – we start to see human figures being used to define letters. They are hard to do, as it is important to maintain some integrity of the human form. If the limbs are twisted too unnaturally, you cannot help but identify with the little figure, and the contortion will seem strained. Occasionally you come across figures like this which are obviously satirical, intended to make you wince or chuckle. But mostly the figures are plausible, suggesting natural postures, or movements in a dance. I have tried to keep to this code of conduct in *Alphabet 12: Humans*. The other thing to notice about the treatment of the human figure in Celtic patterns is that it is usually presented in profile, and this convention extends to the features as well. I had collected a number of studies of the human head from various sources, so the fact that there were several examples of letters with human heads for decorative serifs was a good excuse to draw *Alphabet 11: Human Heads*. This is the only alphabet I had to do twice over. The first time, I fell into the trap of caricaturing my relatives, but thought better of it, and revised my plan.

Introduction

The bird is the oldest motif in Celtic animal art, common to all the schools of the time. It is the most universally widespread motif, and the bird was bent into letterforms in the same way as the lion or the dog, and likewise used just as a serif, or as a filler. I chose the latter option for *Alphabet 15: Birds*, which I drew without any particular traditional source in mind, as birds have long been my favourite Celtic subject.

The last alphabet in this book is representative of the late style that developed in Ireland in the twelfth century. Although the creature is really a very stylized lion, it has absorbed some of that fantastic, heraldic energy which was introduced into Celtic art by the Vikings and which, as Irish Romanesque, was the style that flourished just before the Gothic. I included some examples of the style in *The Dragon and the Griffin*, but the one I had in mind for this alphabet appears as the letter E on page 53 of my painting book, and I built *Alphabet 16: Draco* very closely around that one letter.

I hope that these sixteen Celtic alphabets will be useful as models, and will also inspire fresh adaptation of this blend of Celtic art and letters.

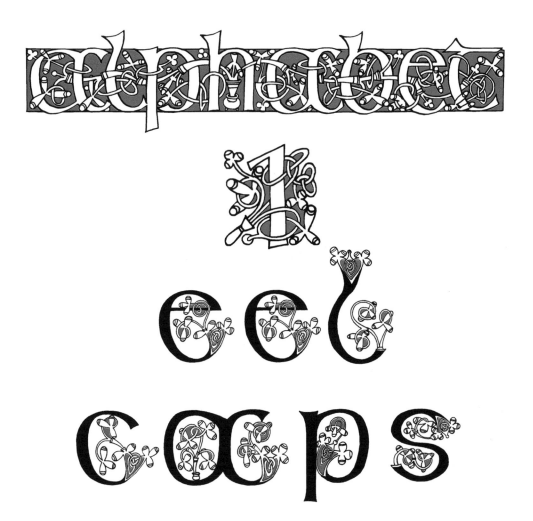

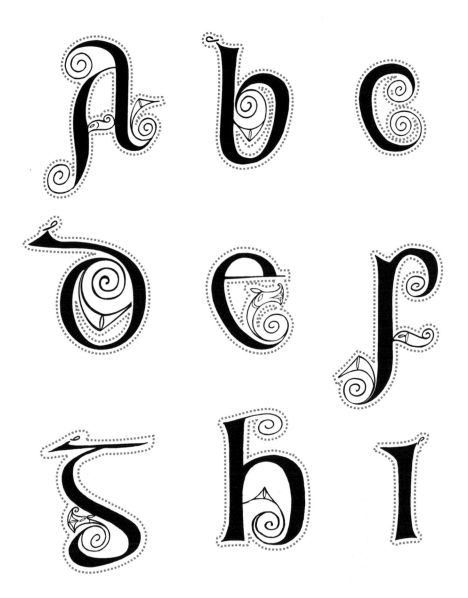

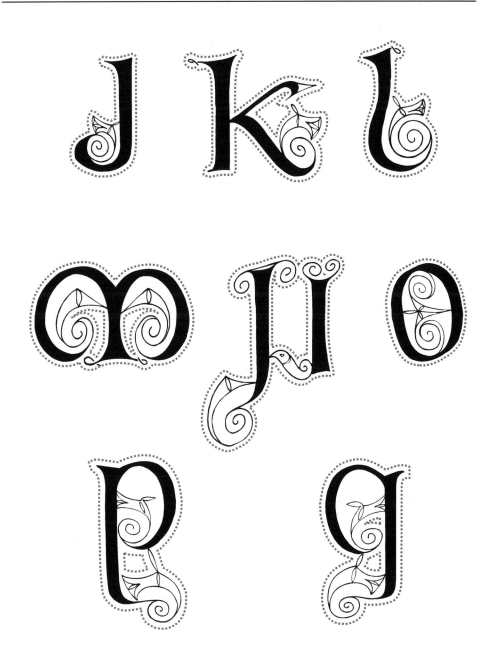

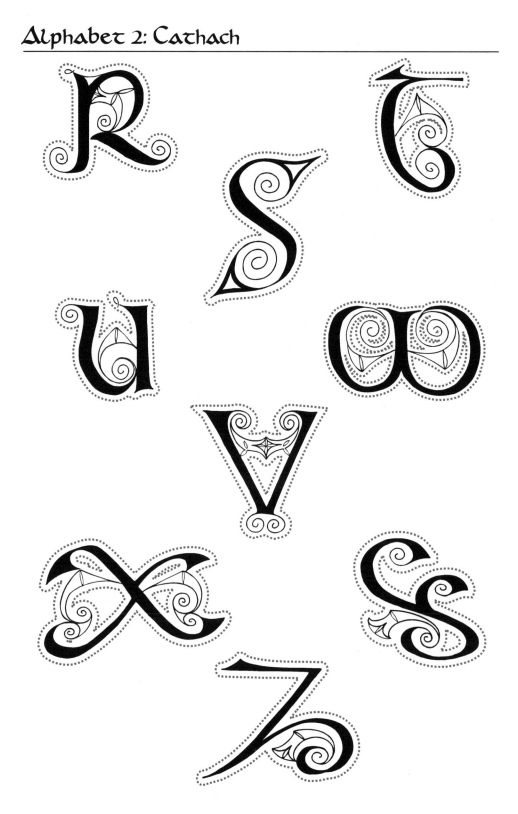

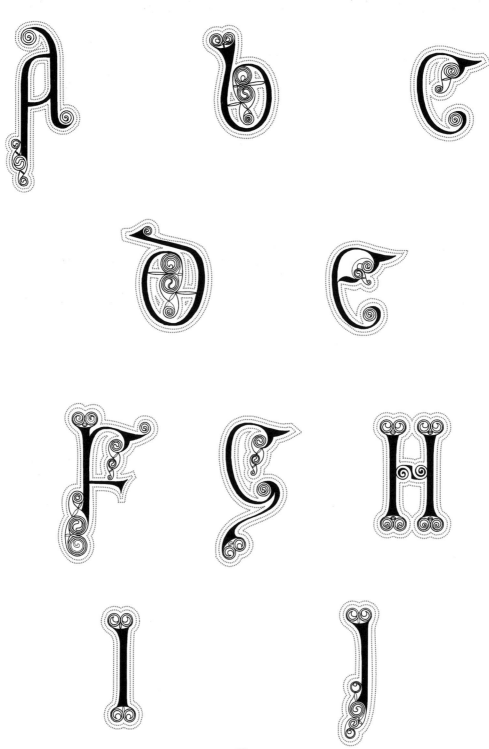

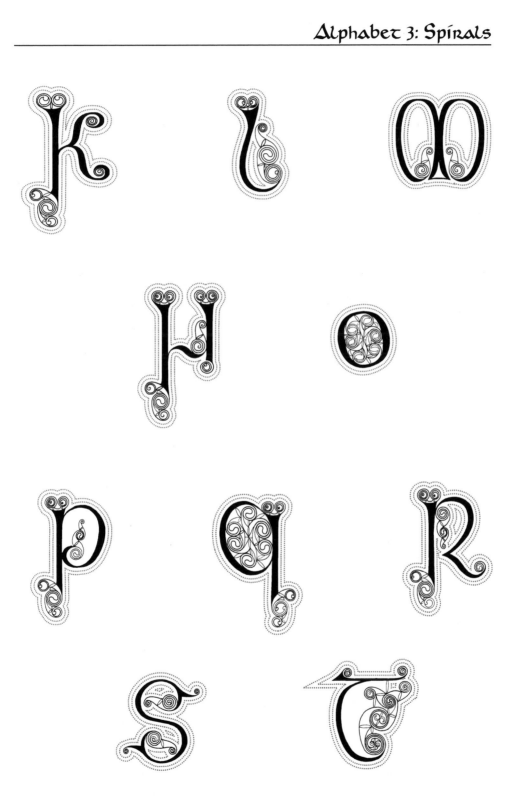

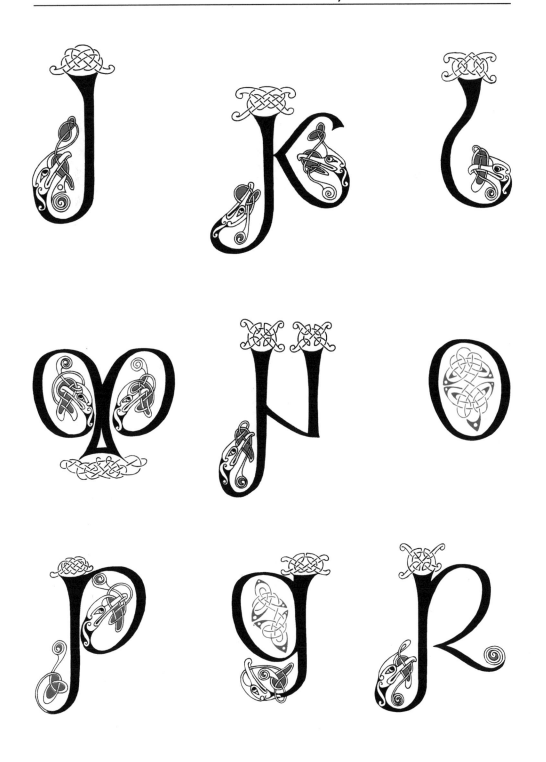

33

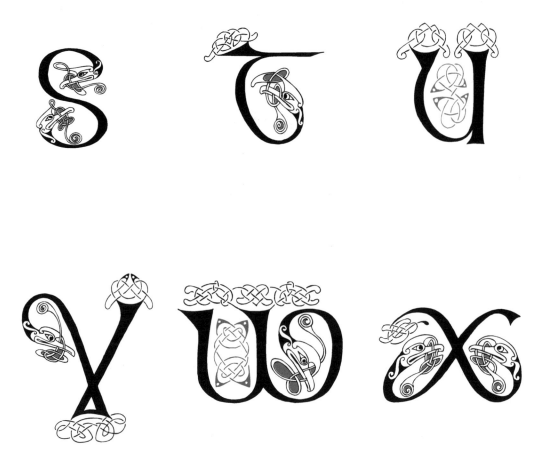

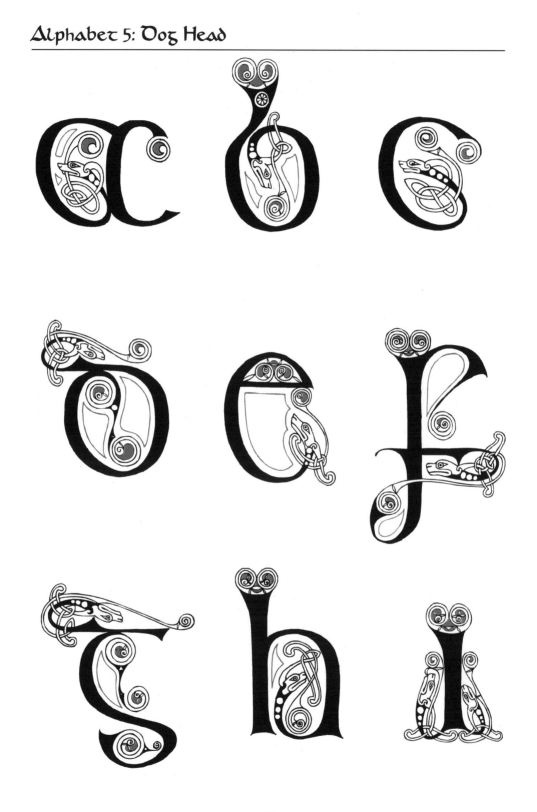

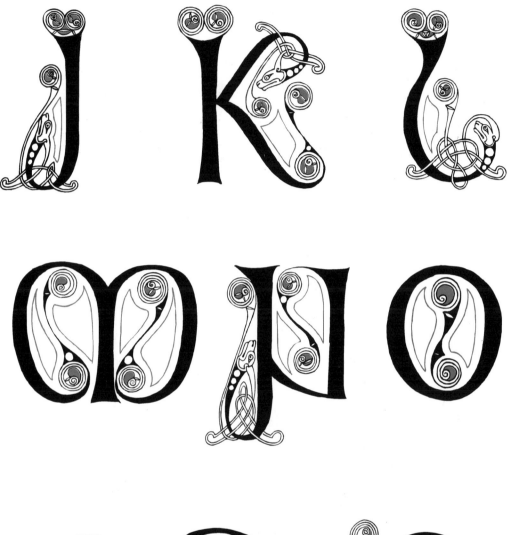

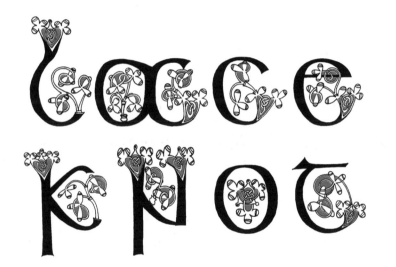

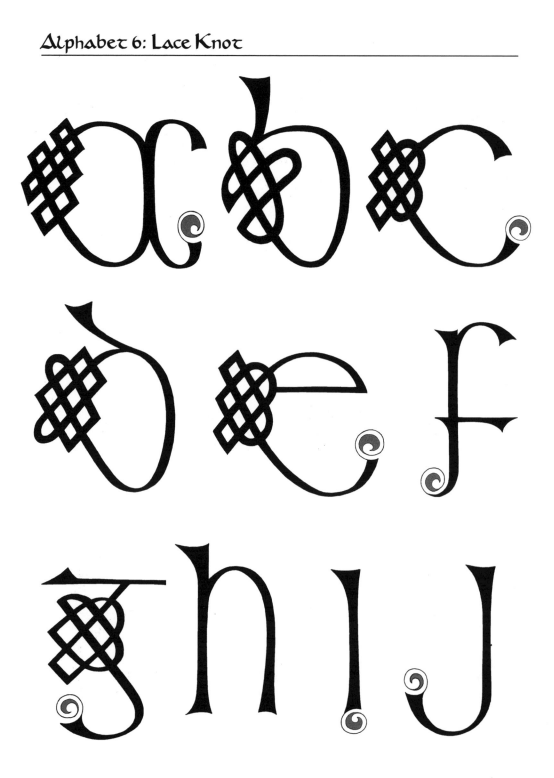

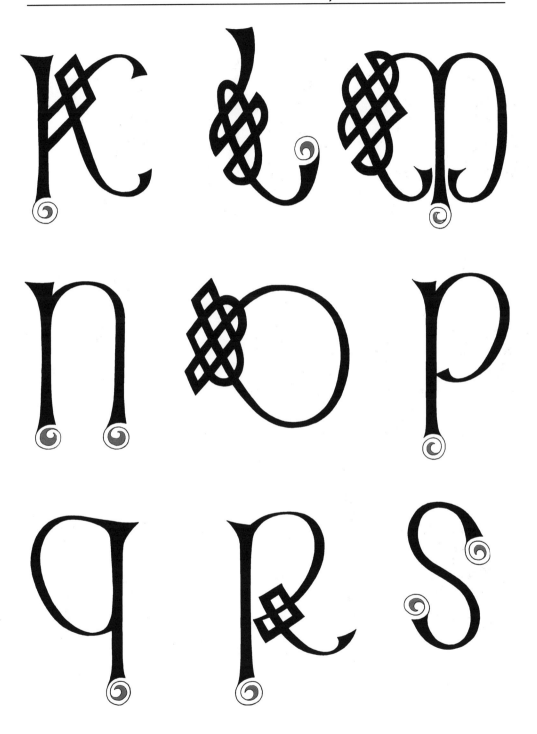

41

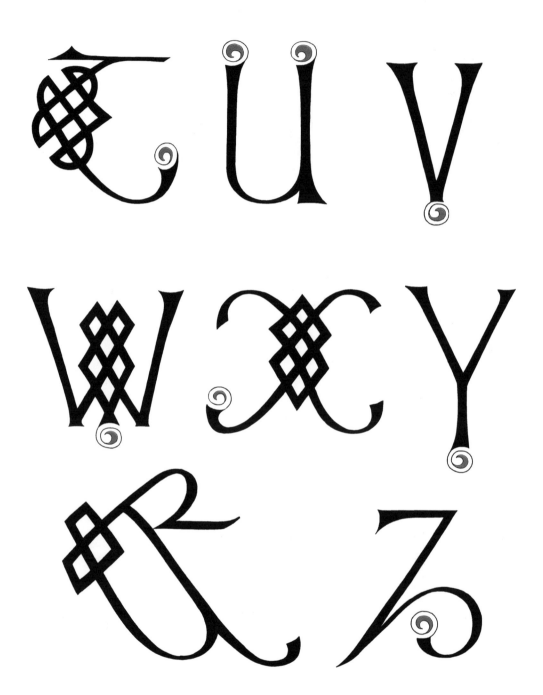

Alphabets 7 dots

45

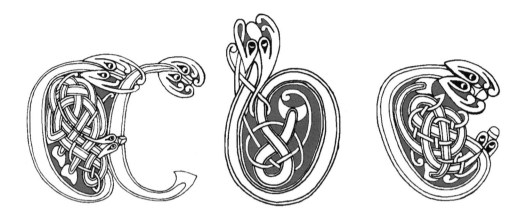

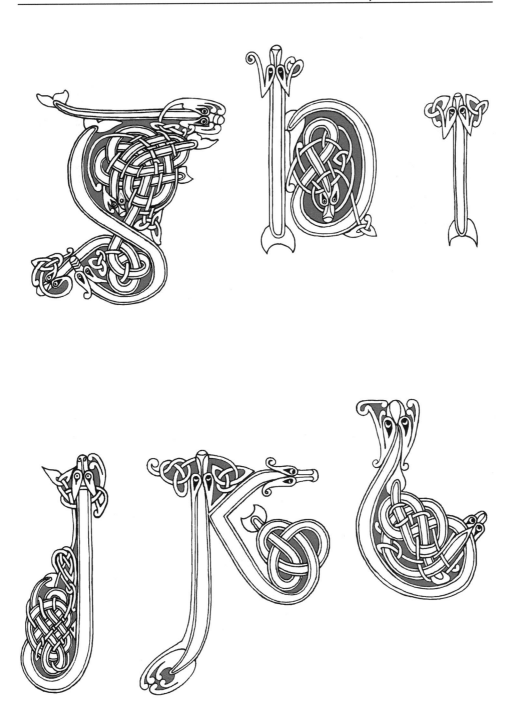

54

55

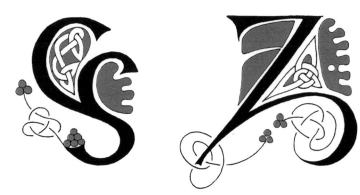

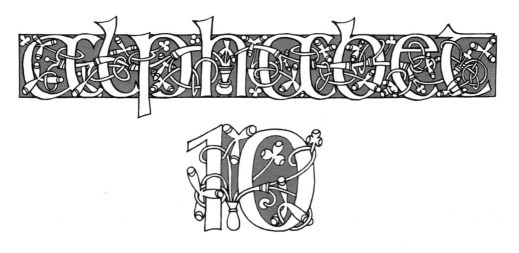

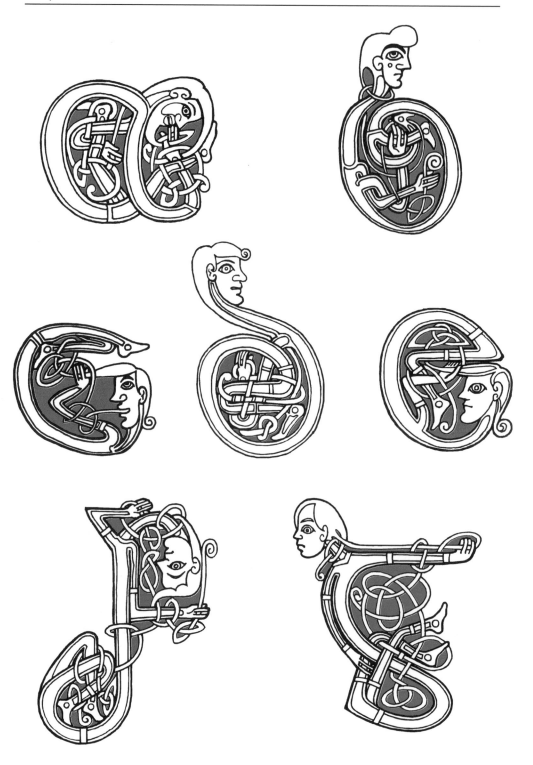

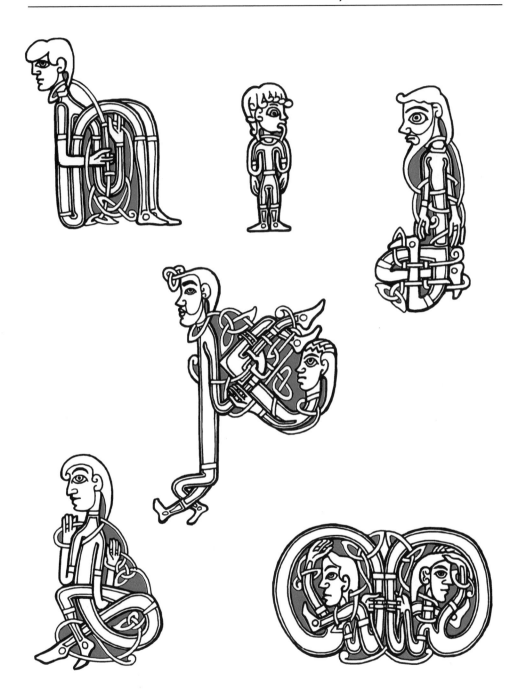

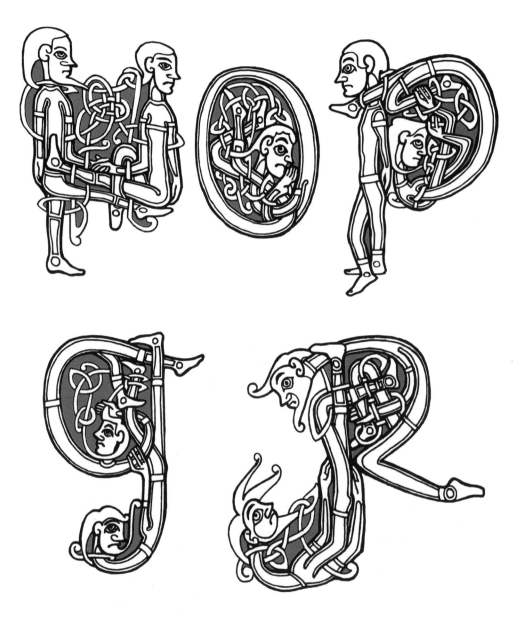

alphabet

13

rabbit
head

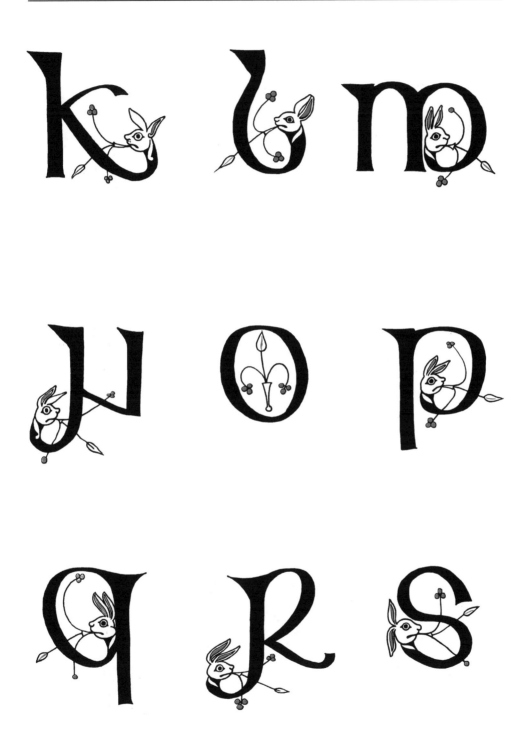

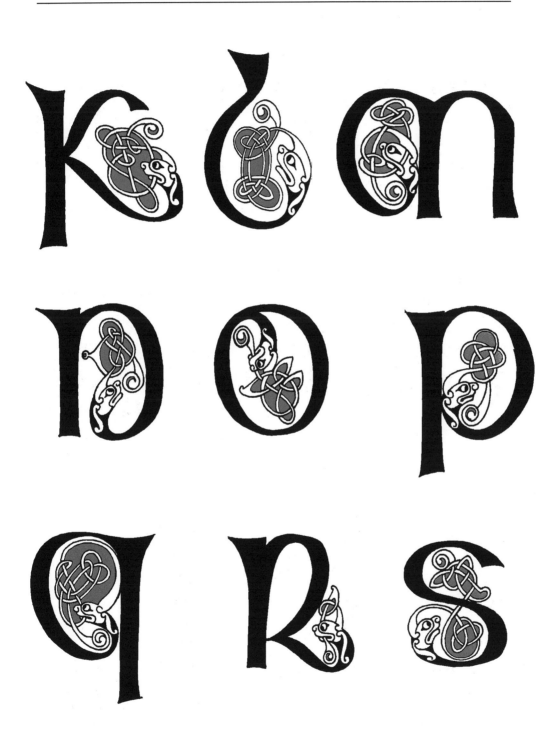

alphabet 15 birds

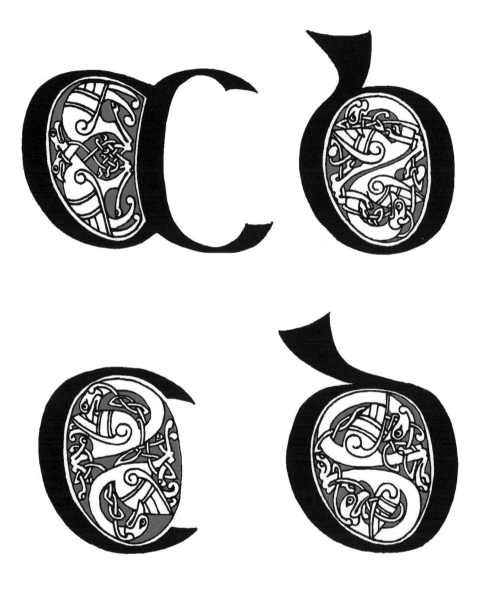

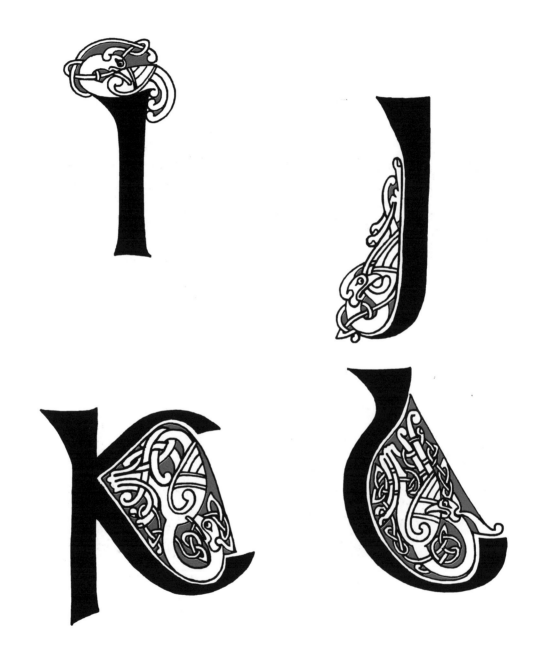

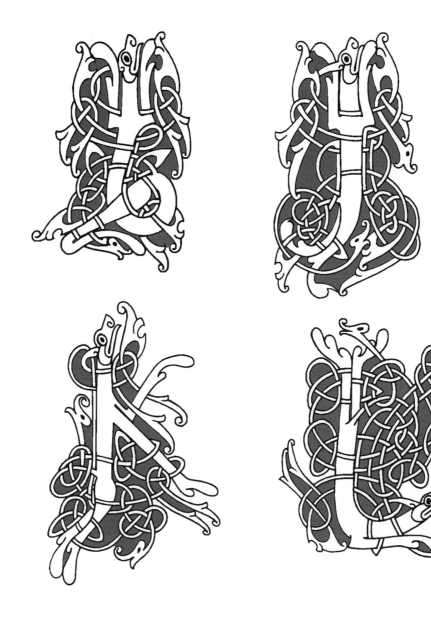

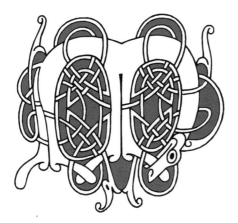

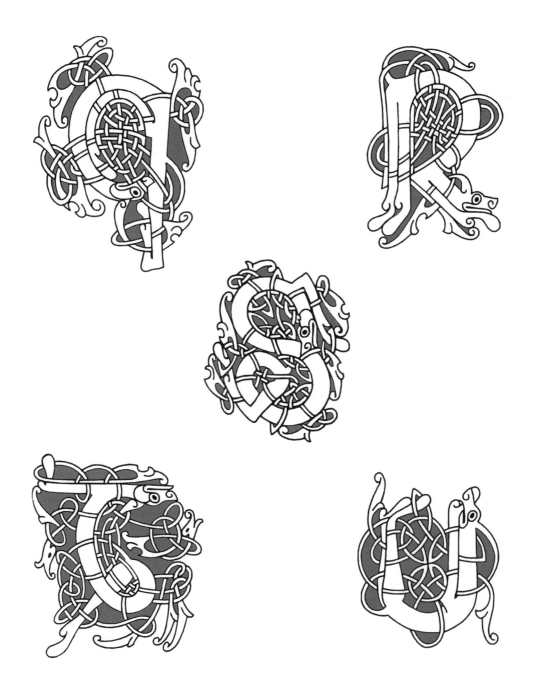

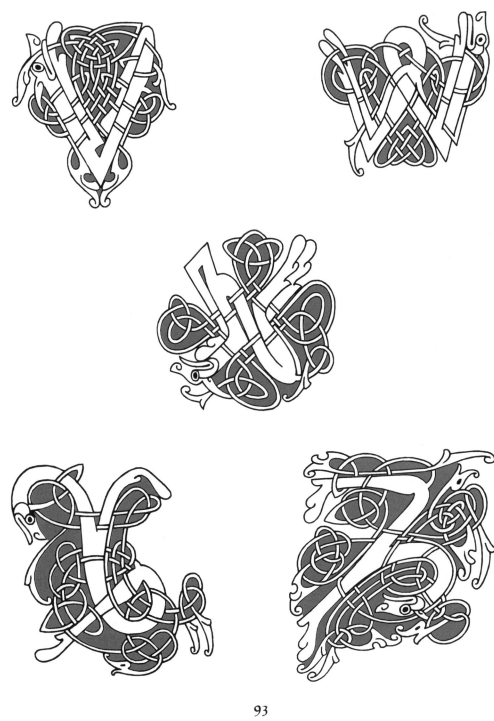

Appendix

Fig. 4: Skeleton Half-Uncials as Drawn with Two Pencils

Here is how to draw the basic Celtic alphabet in skeleton form using two pencils tied together at a slight angle. This is a good way to draw the letters if you want to preserve the feeling of the pen-made script. Many of the alphabets, such as the early ones, and of course those made of animal or human forms, are just drawn with a pencil in the usual way, but it is helpful to know how to construct the uncial letters themselves, as these give Celtic letters their distinctive character. I have already described the order for making the pen strokes of Irish Half-Uncials in chapter 5 of the *Beginner's Manual*, to which this appendix may serve as a footnote.

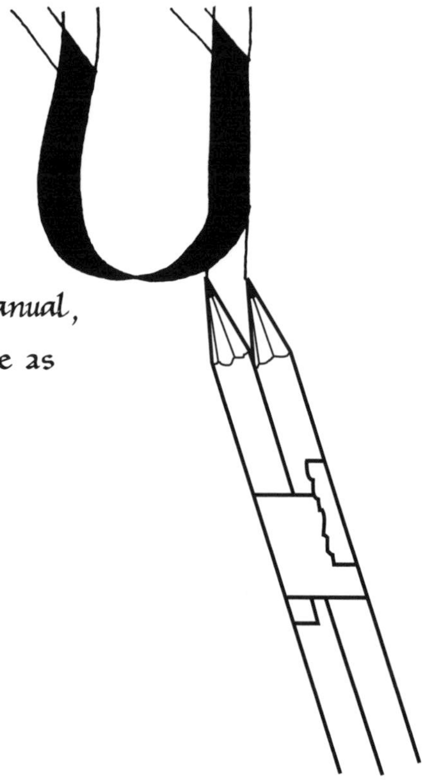

Tape or bind two pencils together as shown so that the right is slightly shorter than the left (if you are right-handed).

Fig. 5: Skeleton Half- Uncials

Appendix

Other books by the author containing examples of decorated letters:

Celtic Design: A Beginner's Manual
Celtic Design: Knotwork
Celtic Design: Animal Patterns
Celtic Design: Illuminated Letters
Celtic Design: Spiral Patterns
Celtic Design: Maze Patterns
Celtic Design: The Dragon and the Griffin
Celtic Design: The Tree of Life

Celtic Patterns Painting Book